Da Ultimate Hookup

FREE THINGS
for all Canadians

Claudette McGowan

Library and Archives Canada Cataloguing in Publication

McGowan, Claudette, 1971-
Da ultimate hookup : free things for all Canadians / Claudette McGowan.

Includes index.
ISBN 978-0-9812114-0-4
1. Free material--Canada--Directories. I. Title.
AG600.M34 2009   011'.03   C2009-901514-5

Cover & Interior Design by Justine Elliott
Editing by T. McLennon

Excelovate

P.O. Box 34021
RPO Hollandview #7
Aurora, Ontario
L4G 0G3

Printed in Canada - Webcom

Disclaimer
Every effort has been made to ensure all information is 100% accurate. It is reasonable to expect some degree of change over time with respect to websites, contact information or the expiration of some offers. The publisher cannot be held responsible for any changes as all offerings are accurate at the time of printing. We encourage you to e-mail feedback to feedback@excelovate.com.

Dedication

I am grateful for all the blessings that have come my way.

Thanks to my family and friends for their endless support.

Special thanks to Ian, Marcus, Savannah and YOU!

Contents

Da Beginning

There are many meanings for the term hookup, so let's be clear from the get go...If you got this book looking for dates with Ashley or Madison, you will be greatly disappointed.

Da Ultimate Hookup is based on the urban meaning of the term hookup, which involves individuals getting access to major discounts or deals. In my opinion, the ultimate hookup is something of value you get for free!

When my parents emigrated from the Caribbean to Canada in the 1960s, they were greeted with extremely cold weather and a whole lot of opportunity. I remember very humble beginnings and frequent moves that saw us living in some pretty rough neighbourhoods within the Greater Toronto Area.

Fast forward to today where I am employed with a major Canadian financial institution working on Bay Street as a Senior Technology Manager. I am also an author, professional life coach, wife, and mother of two kids.

As a young Canadian, I learned a lot of lessons about life struggles. What I also discovered on my journey is that the more money I had, the fewer things I actually paid for. There are so many free things available to us...and many of us don't even have a clue!

Imagine my surprise when I learned that many companies and organizations will send you free things — and all you have to do is ask. You can ask by phone, by posting a letter or by simply sending an e-mail.

Shockingly, many of these companies will actually ship free stuff to your front door! There is no sending $1.00 for shipping and handling, nor do you have to forward them a self-addressed stamped envelope...there is literally no "catch."

After three years of research, I've compiled a comprehensive listing of the organizations and government programs that will give you free food, free entertainment, free products, free services....and free money.

As my parents recognized so many years ago, Canada is a great country with tremendous opportunity for its citizens. If you are a Canadian that wants to save your money and you think you could truly enjoy all the free things life has to offer, don't let this opportunity pass you by.

Get ready for Da Ultimate Hookup!

Money

Let's keep it real. When you got this book, you probably had a bit of doubt because everyone knows there is always a catch. Why would anyone give away free stuff AND seriously, what type of fool do you need to be to hand out free money?

Well, put your doubts to rest. You are about to find out who gives out free money and what you need to do to get your share.

In a show of good faith, I've even decided to get in on the free money game and each week, I will award $100.00 — be sure to check out:

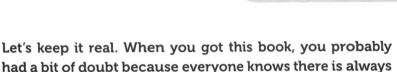

www.daultimatehookup.com

for more details on this hundred dollar hookup.

If you are a lover of American hip hop music, you will know that one of the all time greatest hits is C.R.E.A.M released by the Wu Tang Clan in 1994. C.R.E.A.M is an acronym for Cash Rules Everything Around Me, and it stressed the importance and value of the dollar.

Well, it's 2009 and we are Canadians, but it's still all about the C.R.E.A.M if you want to survive. To make it easier to figure all this free money out, I've placed the free money hookups in three simple categories: grants, tax savings and unclaimed balances.

Get the jump on these programs if you want your share of the free money!

GRANTS

A grant is a sum of money that is given to you based upon a set of conditions and does not need to be paid back.

My younger sister has a lot of opinions so we try to ignore her whenever we can. My search for grants began when she made the statement, "There is no such thing as grants in Canada."

Her statement really irritated me because I was sure that grants were still available. I had even received a grant many, many years ago so I went looking for these long-lost mythical grants.

So, if you happen to apply and receive one of the five grants below, thank my sister; but keep in mind, she will probably take 25 minutes to say "you're welcome."

→ Summer Company Grants

This program allows Ontario students ages 15 – 29 to create their own business with the support of coaches and mentors. If you are a young person with a burning desire to be an entrepreneur, this program awards up to $3000 to get your project off the ground. Apply to the Summer Company program today at:

www.sbe.gov.on.ca/summercompany

→ Canada Council For Arts Grants

The Canada Council offers grants to professional artists in areas such as writing, publishing, theatre, dance and music. This federal government agency works hard to promote the arts but there are several hoops to jump through to actually get one of these grants. If you are a serious artist, this program is for you — posers need not apply. For more details visit them at:

www.canadacouncil.ca/grants

→ Doctoral Studies Grant

This is a specialized program for female students wishing to pursue doctoral studies full time. To receive this Canada Study Grant, you will need to contact your local Provincial/ Territorial assistance office to see if you qualify for this $3000 per year grant. Visit:

www.canlearn.ca/eng/main/help/contact/cao.shtml

→ Gwen Grant

Gwen Grant is a private organization that awards $500 grants to single-mothers in Canada. The application process is very straight-forward and should be completed online.

Single-mothers are asked to share their stories, provide advice and articulate how the $500 will assist them. Based upon their circumstance, Gwen Grant will select up to 10 single-mothers each month. Apply at:

www.gwengrant.org

→ Apprenticeship Incentive Grants

This grant will assist apprentices with expenses such as travel, tools and tuition. If you are interested in becoming a skilled tradesperson, you may be eligible for this $1000 per year grant. To apply, visit the Service Canada website at:

www.servicecanada.gc.ca/eng/goc/aig/apply.shtml

TAX SAVINGS

The best thing I've heard from our government came from Minister Jean-Pierre Blackburn when he said, "you've earned it — claim it!"

While it is always nice to get some cold hard cash in our hands, we need to realize that tax benefits are just as valuable. This money is owed to you, so be sure you go after it with full force. In many cases, these benefits are for regular people who take the bus, work hard to care for their kids and are trying to make ends meet.

When getting your tax return prepared, double-check to ensure that you've applied for every possible savings opportunity.

After all, you've earned it.

→ Public Transit Amount

If you regularly take public transit and are the owner of a monthly transit pass, you can claim this expense on your tax return. Save your transit receipts for yourself, your spouse and any children under 19. The claim is made on line 364 of your tax return.

→ Medical Expenses

Did you know that you can claim medical expenses like laser eye surgery, wigs if you suffer from abnormal hair loss, eyeglasses, wheelchairs, orthodontic work and even air conditioners for those of us that suffer with chronic ailments? Make sure you or your tax preparer account for all medical expenses on line 330 of your tax return.

→ Universal Child Care Benefit

This benefit is an excellent way of providing financial assistance to families with young children. If you are a resident of Canada responsible for a child under six years of age, you may be eligible to receive this monthly $100 benefit per child.

If you already receive the Canada Child Tax Benefit, you will automatically get the Universal Child Care Benefit (UCCB). If you do not receive the Canada Child Tax Benefit, you will need to apply for the UCCB by visiting:

www.cra-arc.gc.ca

→ Tax-Free Savings Account

Imagine a world where you put your money in a savings account and you can withdraw that money whenever you want for whatever you want without being penalized with taxes.

Sounds fairly simple but believe it or not, this is a new and innovative concept for Canada.

If you save your money in an RRSP or put money in an RESP for your kid's education, you will be taxed up the buttocks if you try to take out some of your own cash.

The Tax-Free Savings Account is groundbreaking and every Canadian should open an account immediately and start saving up to $5000 per year tax free.

If you listen to anything I've shared with you in this book, listen to this: start saving your money in a tax free account now. All the major banks offer these accounts, such as BMO – Bank of Montreal, TD Canada Trust, RBC, CIBC and Scotiabank.

For more details, visit your local bank branch or contact the government for a free brochure at 613-995-2855.

→ Children's Fitness Amount

If you watch the news, you hear a lot about childhood obesity. What does that mean? It means our kids are unhealthy and getting fatter with each generation. Keeping our kids healthy is very important and parents can now claim up to $500 for every child under 16.

Let's get our kids back on the fields or in the arenas — the cost of unhealthy children is far more expensive. The government provides criteria for expenses that will be approved, for example the program should require physical activity and span several weeks. Be sure to check out the criteria and make sure you claim the Children's Fitness Amount on line 365 of your tax return.

→ Working Income Tax Benefit

This is a refundable tax credit that provides assistance for low-income individuals that are in the workforce. This tax credit should be claimed on line 453 of your tax return. In general, this credit is for individuals earning less than $12,000 and couples earning less than $21,000. Connect with your tax preparer to see if you are eligible for this credit.

→ Unclaimed Balances

Did you know that as of December 2008, the Bank of Canada has $351 million dollars in unclaimed balances? Apparently, we've become so busy that we've forgotten about our money!

How does your hard earned money get transferred to the Bank of Canada? Well, it's pretty simple, if there has been no owner activity for 10 years, the money is turned over to them to guard your funds until you or a member of your family catch a clue.

You can claim this money if you are the owner or the heir to an estate. Over 90% of these balances are under $1000 but still worth the trouble.

You can get to the bottom of the long lost money mystery by checking online at:

http://www.bankofcanada.ca/en/ucb/index.html

or you can write the Bank of Canada directly at the address below.

Bank of Canada
Unclaimed Balances Services
234 Wellington Street
Ottawa, ON K1A 0G9

Happy treasure hunting!

Dropping
Knowledge On Ya!

Translation: Sharing Some
Interesting Facts About Canada

→ "O Canada" officially became the
national anthem on July 1, 1980.

→ You can get the official Canadian
portrait of Her Majesty Queen
Elizabeth II at:

www.pch.gc.ca

Select Citizenship & Identity then
click The Canadian Monarchy

Rewards Programs

My wallet is jam-packed. Sadly, it is not filled with money. It's overflowing with cards that promised me rewards, points and special memberships.

Guess what? Many of these cards are of very little value and I've decided to toss them. I have one card that no matter when I visit their store, my card has expired.

Of the 22 cards I have in my wallet, I realized that only two actually provide value for my family.

I can't tell you what to do with your cards but I will share which two cards are keepers for me.

The Shoppers Drug Mart Optimum Card rewards you with points every time you shop at Shoppers Drug Mart. From time to time, they offer a special where the points you earn are multiplied by 20. If you can wait, make it a priority to only shop on the 20x the points days.

Once you collect a good amount of points, you can redeem your points and get up to $150 in free products. To apply for your Optimum Card, visit:

www.shoppersdrugmart.ca/english/optimum

The second card that I believe in is the Air Miles Card OR any type of card that rewards you with Air Miles such as the BMO Debit Card. The Air Miles program allows you to collect points as you make your everyday purchases. In turn, you redeem these points for fun things like going to the movies or finally experiencing your dream vacation.

To get more details or to apply for an Air Miles Card, visit:

www.airmiles.ca

Dropping Knowledge On Ya!

Translation: Sharing Some
Interesting Facts About Canada

→ The current population in Canada
  is 33,504,680

→ As of June 1, 2009 Canadians
  wishing to travel to the United States
  will need a passport.

→ People interested in making Canada
  their new home should visit:

www.goingtocanada.gc.ca

  to learn what services and programs
  can assist them throughout the
  transition.

Health

Good health is about your physical, mental, emotional and social well-being. It is important to eat well, exercise, socialize and take time out to rest our bodies.

Here are some valuable free tools and resources that will assist you on your journey to great health.

→ Canada Food Guide

The Canada Food Guide is a Health Canada publication developed to provide a framework for Canadians to make better eating decisions. This guide is available in English, Arabic, Chinese, Spanish and other languages.

To order a free copy of the Canada Food Guide, call: 1 800 622-6232 or download online at:

www.hc-sc.gc.ca

→ Real Age

Do you know your real age? Real Age Inc. is a consumer health company that has an innovative tool that will measure your biological age instead of your calendar age. Visit their website at:

www.realage.com

and select Take the Real Age Test.

When you complete this test, you will receive an assessment and your personalized plan.

→ Physical Activity Guides

The Public Health Agency of Canada offers free physical activity guides for children, teenagers, adults and senior citizens.

These informative guides will help you increase your level of physical activity at home, at school, and at work.

To order your guides, call 1-888-334-9769 or visit:

www.phac-aspc.gc.ca/pau-uap/fitness/order.html

→ The Sensible Guide To A Healthy Pregnancy

This handy pregnancy guide will provide you with vital information to prepare and assist with having a healthy pregnancy. Expectant parents will find the 10-month pregnancy calendar extremely valuable and informative. To order this Government of Canada publication, call 1 800 622-6232 or visit:

http://www.healthycanadians.gc.ca

→ Breast Cancer CD

Vassar College offers a free CD that tackles the environmental risks of breast cancer. This CD was designed to inform men and women about the various risks including reproductive history, lifestyle and genetic factors.

To order a copy of the CD, visit:

http://erbc.vassar.edu

→ Meditation CD

Meditation & Transformation offers a free Meditation CD.

Meditation is an alternative therapy or process used by people to transform their minds and attain greater relaxation in their pursuit for better health. People who meditate report feeling higher levels of clarity and overall happiness. To order a free CD, visit:

www.meditationandtransformation.com/optin.htm

Food

In order to survive, we all need to eat. Thankfully, there are several wonderful restaurants in Canada where you can eat free on special days. Some of these days are just for kids and for the rest of us, these restaurants will hook us up on our birthday or when we join their online clubs. It is important to note that these programs can change at any time so please give them a call, visit their website or get on my mailing list at:

www.daultimatehookup.com

for the latest and greatest in food freebies.

The top seven Eat Free Programs are as follows:

→ East Side Mario's

East Side Mario's provides Italian cuisine at affordable prices. It is very family friendly and the servings are generous.

They currently offer a Kid's Eat Free special with the purchase of each adult entrée. In my neighbourhood, kids eat free on Monday if they are 10 and under. Please visit their website at:

www.eastsidemarios.com

to find out what day kids eat free at your local restaurant.

→ Red Lobster

Red Lobster is a casual dining restaurant that specializes in seafood. When you visit their website at:

www.redlobster.com

and join the Fresh Catch Club, you will be surprised with a free birthday gift to help you celebrate.

→ Boston Pizza

Boston Pizza is a full-service restaurant that specializes in pizza, pasta and great appetizers. These restaurants are known for friendly service and great sports bars. When you visit them online and sign up for their email club, you will receive great offers along with a free appetizer/starter. If you are above the age of majority, visit Boston Pizza today at:

www.bostonpizza.com

to join the e-mail club.

→ Holiday Inn

When families decide to stay at a US or Canadian Holiday Inn hotel, they should take advantage of the great Kids Eat Free offer for kids 12 and under.

This program is for registered guests and they limit the number of kids at four per dining family. For more details, visit their website at:

www.holidayinn.com

and click on Customer Care followed by the About Holiday Inn to find out about the many features such as Kids Eat Free and Kids Stay Free.

→ Denny's

Denny's is a family restaurant known for their fantastic breakfast meals. They are currently offering a Kids Eat Free program on Tuesdays and Saturdays. Denny's even goes the extra mile in providing a free birthday meal on your special day when you dine with a friend who purchases a meal. For more details or a list of their locations, visit Denny's in person or online at:

www.dennys.ca

→ Montana's

For homestyle cooking and delicious ribs and steaks, Montana's Cookhouse is the place to be.

Montana's offers a free appetizer when you sign up online for Cookhouse News; visit at:

www.montanas.ca/eng/contest.php

and kids under 10 enjoy a free meal when they join the Cookhouse Birthday Club at:

www.montanas.ca/eng/kids.php

→ Pizza Pizza

Join the Pizza Pizza Kid's Club by signing up online at:

www.pizzapizza.ca

Kid's Club members will receive a birthday card delivered to their home, a slice of pizza and a drink in honour of their birthday. This program is currently offered in Quebec and Ontario for children under 12 years of age.

To receive the birthday card on time, please ensure you have signed up prior to the 15th day of the preceding month.

Our sources tell us that restaurants like Jack Astors, Casey's and The Keg offer special treats on your birthday. The bottom line is to be aware that many restaurants offer free food promotions and it is your job to visit their websites or give them a call.

What do you have to lose? Start taking advantage of these free food offers and keep your money in your pocket.

FOOD BANKS

As Canadians we are very fortunate to have food banks across the country available to families in dire need. Food banks are located throughout our communities and serve a critical role in eliminating hunger in Canada.

Food Banks Canada represents food banks in every province and they are collectively committed to a hunger-free Canada. For more information on food banks in Canada, visit:

www.foodbankscanada.ca

FOOD BANKS CANADA MEMBERS

CAFB - British Columbia Branch
Phone: 604-876-3601

Association Québécoise Des Banques Alimentaires Et Des Moissons
Phone: 450-444-4040

Alberta Food Bank Network Association
Phone: 780-488-9719
Toll free: 866-251-2326

www.afbna.ca/

New Brunswick Association of Food Banks
Phone: 506-457-1788

Food Banks of Saskatchewan Corporation
Phone: 306-937-5505

Feed Nova Scotia
Phone: 902-457-1900

www.feednovascotia.ca/

Manitoba Association of Food Banks
Phone: 204-982-3663

P.E.I. Association of Food Banks
Phone: 902-892-7092

Ontario Association of Food Banks
Phone: 416-656-4100

www.oafb.ca/

Community Food Sharing Association of Newfoundland & Labrador
Phone: 709-722-0130

www.cfsa.nf.net/

Babies

Every baby is a blessing, it takes a village, children are the future, etc...etc...etc.... Bottom line, we need to take care of our kids from the moment they enter our lives. That means, healthy eating and a good dose of knowledge to avoid the baby mama drama. Here are the top 10 free things available for new parents:

→ Similac Welcome Addition Club

This program offers a great welcome kit with free samples of baby formula, coupons and other goodies. To join the club, you can sign up online at:

www.abbott.ca

Select your preferred language (English/French) and choose the option for the Similac Welcome Addition Club.

This program also provides a contact telephone number: 1-800-518-CLUB (2582).

→ Johnson & Johnson New Parent Pack

Johnson & Johnson are leaders in personal care products for all family members, especially babies. To learn more about their full suite of products visit them online at:

www.jnjcanada.com

To order your New Parent Pack, call 1-877-223-9807. The parent pack includes samples, coupons and general information.

→ Nestle Baby Program

With over 140 years of experience in the infant food industry, Nestle is committed to the health and wellness of both mother and baby. They have an exceptional website that is full of great tools and information for new parents at:

www.nestle-baby.ca

In addition to their great online presence, they offer the Nestle Baby Program. This free program includes a very handy backpack, a subscription to their magazine and free samples. To join this program you can call Nestle at 1-800-387-5536 or sign up online at:

www.nestle-baby.ca

As a mother of two, I cannot praise them enough for their Good Start formula — way to go Nestle!

→ Welcome Wagon

C'mon, doesn't the name Welcome Wagon sound kinda fun and inviting! As a new parent, you may even welcome some adult company for a change!

The Welcome Wagon is a free greeting organization with programs for new moms. They will pay you a quick visit and leave you with free goodies, coupons and information packages to help you with your newborn.

The Welcome Wagon began in 1930 and they haven't lost any steam since! Go online to:

www.welcomewagon.ca

to schedule a home visit or attend one of their local Welcome Wagon Baby Showers. You'll love it!

→ Proctor & Gamble (Pampers)

By the time your kid turns three, you will become an expert at diapers, just when they will no longer need them. The good folks at Proctor & Gamble offer free goodies when you join online at:

www.pampers.ca

By joining you will receive their newsletter, a personalized web experience based upon your child's age and occasional free samples. Pampers.ca is also offering the Gifts to Grow Program that rewards you with points when you purchase their products.

→ Kimberly-Clark (Huggies)

Every parent has a diaper favourite — mine is Huggies. I have a girl and a boy and in both cases, let's just say Huggies can weather ANY storm! My kids have stress tested many diapers and in our family, Huggies is the clear winner. As I look forward to aging gracefully, I hope Kimberly-Clark has a similar offering for my golden years!

By joining the Huggies Baby Network, you will receive free samples, coupons, activity books and their parenting newsletter. Visit online at:

www.huggies.com

or call 1-800-544-1847 and join the Huggies Baby Network today.

→ Pull-Ups Potty Training DVD

I learned very quickly that discussion and reasoning were not the best ways to convince my child to use the potty. We got the DVD and after watching it three times, my son started using the potty, just like that! Save yourself money and hassle by getting a free copy of the PULL-UPS Big Kid Central Potty Training Success DVD. This DVD has some cool ways to make potty training a fun experience for the parents and the kiddies! Visit this website to get your free DVD:

www.pull-ups.com

→ Goodnights

Goodnights Sleep Pants provide protection overnight for children prone to bedwetting. It is estimated that 20% of children aged four to 12 wet the bed and the key message for parents to remember is that bedwetting is not linked to laziness.

Reach out to your doctor and you will learn that there are many factors and causes that are typically outgrown over time. For a free sample of Goodnights Sleep Pants visit:

www.goodnites.com

→ Heinz Baby Club

Our friends at Heinz have been making baby food for over 70 years. As the number one choice for Canadian mothers, Heinz is a name we can all trust. The Heinz Baby Club offers an e-newsletter, eco-friendly reusable shopping bag, coupons, special offers and samples delivered to your home. Visit their website at:

www.heinzbaby.com

and sign up for the Heinz Baby Club when your child is about two months old. Mailings begin when your child reaches four months of age.

→ Twins? Triplets? Octuplets!!!

If you are fortunate enough to be blessed with more than one bundle of joy - congratulations! There are many companies that also want to wish you well by giving you a few freebies. Check out companies like Evenflo and Enfamil for their multiple birth programs. You can call them or visit their websites and select the Contact Us page to make a request.

www.evenflo.com   1-937-773-3971

www.enfamil.ca   1 800 361-6323

Kids

Kids are major consumers in the marketplace and many companies are targeting kids in their ads. The marketing companies figured out a long time ago that Mom and Dad are no longer running the household!

Here are some great products and services available for kids:

→ Kids Help Phone

This amazing service allows our kids to get counseling, express themselves and seek information on topics that are on their minds.

Kids can reach out by phone at 1-800-668-6868 or online by visiting:

www.kidshelpphone.ca

What makes this service special is that it is anonymous, confidential and open 24 hours.

If kids are not comfortable calling, they can use the online searchable database to get access to information on topics such as family life, school, friendship, health, dating, and violence to name a few.

This is not just a service for troubled kids; it is an excellent tool for every kid.

→ Music For Kids

Kids have a lot of choices when it comes to what type of music they listen to. It is sometimes difficult to determine what CDs or MP3s are appropriate. Free Kids' Music solves this problem by providing a catalogue of free music specifically geared toward kids. Visit:

www.freekidsmusic.com

to create a CD or download music made for kids.

→ Free Tokens

Chuck E. Cheese is a fun place for kids to have a good time. They have games, prizes, rides, shows and lots of pizza. My five-year-old son thinks Chuck E. Cheese is the best place on earth and will do anything to be there as often as possible.

If you plan to visit and dine at Chuck E. Cheese, you need to take advantage of their free token offers. The two promotions are the Rewards Calendar and Token for Grade Programs.

Kids will receive free tokens for their accomplishments relating to things like good manners, progress with reading, sleeping through the night, and cleaning their room. The Tokens for Grade program requires your child to bring in their report card and receive tokens based on their academic performance.

For more details, visit:

www.chuckecheese.com

→ Free Piggy Bank

The Children's Education Fund Inc. offers a free Piggy Bank for your kid when you visit online and complete a quick form. This company markets Registered Education Savings Plans and they will contact you by phone to set up an appointment to deliver your free gift.

In addition to the Piggy Bank, they also offer other free items for kids such as drawing boards, fork & spoon sets, two-handled cups and child identification kits. At this time, only one item per household is allowed and this offer is while quantities last.

To receive a complimentary gift from the Children's Education Fund, visit:

www.cefi.ca

→ Kids Helmet Safety DVD

Visit:

www.morellkelly.com

to order a copy of the Lidz on Kidz DVD. Morell Kelly is a personal injury law firm that works to raise helmet safety awareness. They partner with the Brain Injury Association and educate children and families about the importance of wearing helmets when engaged in activities such as biking.

→ Lego Magazine

Do you love Lego? Ok, maybe you don't love it, but do you like it? Here is an opportunity to get Lego magazine for two years, absolutely free! Order your free subscription by calling 1 866-534-6258 or visiting:

www.lego.ca

and click the link for the Free Lego Magazine. You will also have the option of choosing whether you want the English or French version delivered to your home.

Dropping Knowledge On Ya!

Translation: Sharing Some Interesting Facts About Canada

→ You can show your support for our Canadian troops by sending them a message at:

www.forces.gc.ca/site/commun/
message/message-add-ajout-eng.asp

→ The Government of Canada offers a free guide outlining the services available for People with Disabilities and their families – visit:

www.pwd-online.ca

Pets

Pets are animals that live with humans and provide companionship, security and for the most part, pleasure.

According to a recent study, more than half of Canadian households have a cat or dog. The study confirmed the most common household pets are cats, dogs, birds, fish and reptiles.

When it comes to pets, my top five freebies will hook you up on things like getting your own pet, animal care guides, pet food and animal training videos.

→ Free Pets at Kijiji

Kijiji is a free online classified service that is used for many purposes. One of the classified sections enables pet owners to give or donate pets. In researching for this book, I learned that people give pets away for a variety of reasons.

The most popular reason for giving a pet away involves a change in personal circumstance. The three reasons I heard frequently relate to the birth of a baby, job relocation and my all-time favourite, when someone falls in love with a pet-hater and is forced to decide — me or the pet! I'd probably choose the pet!

Check out:

www.kijiji.com

to experience the sheer joy, amusement and unconditional love of your very own pet.

→ Vegetarian Starter Kits from PETA

People for the Ethical Treatment of Animals (PETA) is the largest animal rights organization in the world. With over two million members they are focused on things like animal rescue, public education and eliminating animal cruelty.

PETA offers several free products such as Vegetarian Starter Kits, stickers and information on how you can help animals.

If you are a young person, check out the PETA2 website at:

www.peta2.com

This youthful site has great videos, contests and freebies.

For the grown folks, visit:

www.peta.org

to get informed and sign up for your recipe-filled Vegetarian Starter Kit.

→ E-Cards From Petfinder

Petfinder is an online database filled with over 200,000 animals waiting to be adopted. This organization has placed over 12 million animals since they opened their doors in 1995.

If you are a pet-lover or considering the companionship of a pet, you have to visit:

www.petfinder.com

Their informative website is full of advice, training, online videos and games. One of the useful tools on this website is the free e-card service. This service allows you to send pet-inspired e-cards for every occasion. Check it out at:

www.petfinder.com/tools/ecards

→ Free Puppy Kit

The Purina MyPuppy program will assist puppy owners in caring for their new addition. Join this program at:

www.mypuppy.ca

and you will receive an in-depth care guide, a puppy ID tag, a coupon for a free bag of Purina puppy food and a Health Chart to help you monitor your puppy's development.

→ Free Kitten Kit

All kittens need tender loving care and the Purina MyKitten program provides an exceptional starter pack for new kitten owners. When you join this program you will receive an adorable ID tag, a comprehensive care guide, Purina Pet Advisor contact information and a coupon for a free bag of Purina kitten food. For more details, visit:

www.mykitten.ca

Mail Order Catalogues

Why would anyone want to buy anything through mail order? The first catalogues in Canada surfaced during the 1880s.

With the real-time razzle dazzle of the Internet, one would think the mail order business would have joined the dinosaur population in extinction.

Shockingly, mail order catalogues continues to thrive for the following reasons: they allow us to dream and anticipate, they provide convenience, they cater to specific markets (e.g., fisherman, gardeners and big-boned women), they allow for privacy, and most importantly, they are far easier to bring into the washroom than a laptop.

There are thousands of free consumer catalogues that are delivered to major centres and remote regions across Canada. A good website to checkout for Canadian catalogues is:

www.shopincanada.com

My top ten favourites are not all Canadian companies but the following free catalogues are available for all Canadians.

→ Victoria's Secret

Victoria's Secret specializes in lingerie and beauty products. Their headquarters are located in Columbus, Ohio and they have over 1000 stores in the US. Limited Brands is the owner of Victoria's Secret and Canada's #1 lingerie brand, La Senza.

This catalogue is known for its glamorous supermodels and provocative lingerie. You can get this catalogue by visiting:

www.victoriassecret.com

and selecting the option to request a catalogue.

→ Canada Post

Canada Post offers two informative publications for stamp collectors. They are aptly titled Collections and Details. Collections highlights unique products and Details shares specifics on design techniques and the history of stamp products.

Visit:

www.canadapost.ca/personal/productsservices/collect/default.aspx

to subscribe for Details and/or Collections.

→ Canadian Wedding Treasures

This Canadian company has operated for almost 40 years and they specialize in wedding invitations, announcements, scrolls and thank you cards. They provide fast service and deliver a quality product. To request a catalogue and/or invitation samples, call them at 1-800-387-0983 or visit online:

www.canadianwedding.ca

→ Hunter Douglas

If you really want to make a difference in the look and feel of your home, try experimenting with your windows. Hunter Douglas makes window shadings and they offer a free book/ catalogue that will provide hundreds of inspiring ideas. To order this free book, visit Hunter Douglas online at:

www.hunterdouglas.com/designingwindows

→ J. Crew

This American brand is known for providing sophisticated yet functional clothing for all members of the family. J. Crew has received a lot of attention lately as it is reported to be a favourite of the US First Lady Michelle Obama and her two daughters. Both girls were outfitted by J. Crew at the most remarkable inauguration in US history.

To request a catalogue, visit J. Crew online at:

www.jcrew.com

and your catalogue should arrive in three weeks.

→ Vesey's Gardeners

Vesey's has been in the gardening mail order business since 1939 and they are located in York, Prince Edward Island.

With over seven decades of providing gardening advice, products and services, Vesey's has a long-standing tradition of distributing high-quality seeds to gardeners.

This free subscription entitles you to several Vesey publications, including a planting guide and seed catalogue. This is a must-have for those who value and treasure their gardens. Visit online to order your free catalogue today:

www.veseys.com/ca/en/

→ Esoteric Hydroponics

Did you know that 90% of the fresh-cut flowers in the UK are hydroponically grown? Did you know that hydroponics enables a gardener to grow at least twice the yield in a smaller space at a much faster rate? Esoteric Hydroponics aims to bring nature and technology together. For more details on hydroponics, contact Esoteric Hydroponics for your free catalogue and CD Rom:

www.1-hydroponics.co.uk

→ Musician's Friend

Musician's Friend is a US company that has the honour of being one of the world's biggest direct sellers of musical products. They strive to offer the best price and selection to musicians worldwide. For musical instruments, DJ products as well as mixing and lighting goods, they are well worth checking out. Request your free catalogue by calling 800-391-8762 or filling out a form online at:

www.musiciansfriend.com

Note their hours of business are 4:00 AM PST to 11:00 PM PST.

→ Tiger Direct

This is a personal favourite because I find they offer the best price when it comes to technology. Don't spend a cent on computers or electronics until you have checked out the prices at TigerDirect.

When you request a catalogue, you will also be placed on their mailing list. If you love tech toys and gadgets, you seriously need to be on their mailing list. Visit:

www.tigerdirect.ca

and request your free catalogue. This is a hookup you shouldn't pass up!

→ Northland Fishing Tackle

The Northland Fishing Tackle company designs exclusive products to help you catch more fish — if you're into that kinda stuff! Their innovative approach has resulted in Northland becoming a favourite among fishermen worldwide. Their catalogue not only includes their product line but also incorporates must-have tips, tricks and techniques. To order your 96-page catalogue and fishing guide go to:

www.northlandtackle.com/Catalog/freecatalog.taf

or visit their main page at:

www.northlandtackle.com/

@ School

Scholarships

In Canada, millions of dollars are available for students to help pay for college and university. This financial aid comes in the form of scholarships, grants, bursaries and prizes from private donors and the Canadian government.

Sadly, some organizations report that students are not applying for these awards and as a result, free money for students goes unclaimed each year. I conducted an unofficial survey of 50 students and learned that 82% believed scholarships are hard to get and 90% reported that only students with exceptional grades receive scholarships.

So, let's set the record straight, you don't need high marks to get a scholarship.

A scholarship is basically a financial grant to assist students with tuition, books and living costs while studying. While it is true that some scholarships are awarded based on academic achievement, there are just as many scholarships awarded based upon financial need. Other untapped resources include scholarships provided to students based upon their ethnic background or their relationship with a company, association or religious organization.

Two great websites that enable you to access their free scholarship databases are:

www.aucc.ca

and:

www.scholarshipscanada.com

Here are 10 scholarship opportunities that Canadian students and parents need to check out in order to get hooked up on free money for college and university:

1. Canada Millennium Excellence Awards (1000 awards)
2. Kin Canada Bursaries (52 bursaries)
3. Monsanto Canada Scholarships (50 scholarships)
4. Wendy's Classic Achiever Scholarship (30 scholarships)
5. Youth in Motion: Top 20 under Twenty (20 awards)
6. TD Canada Trust Scholarship (20 scholarships)
7. Miller Thomson Foundation (200 scholarships)
8. BBPA Scholarships (varies)
9. Leonard Foundation Financial Assistance (140 awards)
10. Learning Disability Scholarships (varies)

→ Canada Millennium Excellence Awards

This program awards over 1000 Canadian students for leadership, innovation community service as well as academic performance.

To begin the process you have to complete an application, submit short essays and provide references. For more information, visit Canada Millennium Scholarship Foundation online at:

www.millenniumscholarships.ca

or by calling them at 1-514-284-7230.

→ Kin Canada Bursaries

Kin Canada is an all-Canadian organization dedicated to serving the community through positive values and national pride. Kin Canada awards $1000 bursaries to students based on financial need, community service and knowledge of Kin Canada. To get more information or apply, visit online at:

www.bursary.ca

→ Monsanto Canada Scholarships

If you intend to enter a program in agriculture or forestry and have some family farming background, this is the scholarship for you. Monsanto is an innovative agricultural company that uses modern biotechnology tools in order to improve a seed's ability to grow.

Log on to their website at:

www.monsanto.ca

to apply and be considered for this opportunity scholarship.

→ Wendy's Classic Achiever Scholarships

The Wendy's Classic Achiever Scholarship recognizes graduating high school students who have delivered academically and in their communities. If you are a winner when it comes to high marks, that is not enough; a classic achiever must also give back to the community. Sound like you? Apply online at:

www.wendysclassicachiever.ca

and keep in mind that you will have to prepare a 300-word essay answering a very insightful question. Hey, if you can't do it, who can!

→ Youth In Motion

Youth in Motion is a Canadian charitable organization dedicated to helping youth thrive. If you are under 20 and have demonstrated significant leadership, innovation and achievement apply online for this $5000 award at:

www.top20under20.ca

→ TD Canada Trust Scholarship

The TD Canada Trust Scholarship for Community leaders is for students that are making a difference. If you have demonstrated leadership by challenging injustice, this scholarship was created to recognize your efforts. This program will cover your entire post-secondary program — up to $70,000 toward your expenses — and it also includes opportunities to build a meaningful relationship with TD with paid summer employment, mentoring and networking events. If you are graduating with a grade of 75% or higher, and are truly a community leader, visit:

www.tdcanadatrust.com/scholarship

→ Miller Thomson Foundation

Miller Thomson is a full-service law firm serving clients across Canada. The Miller Thomson Foundation is committed to recognizing and supporting the achievement of young Canadians.

This scholarship recognizes 200 superstars. You have to truly shine in the classroom, at extracurricular activities and in the community to win this one! If you think you've got it going on, apply online at:

www.millerthomson.com

→ Black Business Professional Association

The Black Business Professional Association works to advance the Canadian black community through specialized programs. They offer several scholarships for young people and host the spectacular Harry Jerome Awards each year. To be considered for a scholarship or award, criteria is based upon several factors such as financial need, Canadian citizenship, high academic achievement and demonstrated service to the black community. Visit:

www.bbpa.org

for more information or call the BBPA at 416-504-4097.

→ Leonard Foundation Financial Assistance

This foundation grants awards of $1000 to over 120 undergrad students each year. The founder of this program was committed to assisting students who demonstrated true financial need. It is also important to note that preference is given to the daughters or sons of ordained clergy, licensed teachers and Canadian military personnel. Visit the Leonard Foundation online at:

www.leonardfnd.org

→ Learning Disability Association of Canada

The Learning Disabilities Association of Canada offers scholarships to individuals with learning disabilities such as dyscalculia (math), dysgraphia (writing) and dyspraxia (motor skills development). Visit:

www.ldac-taac.ca/Scholarships/scholarships-e.asp

to apply for specialized scholarships like the Doreen Kronick Scholarship or the Carol Thomson Memorial Fund for Students with Learning Disabilities.

→ Honourable Mentions

Check out these other great scholarships by visiting their websites, the trick is to find the best programs that fit your character and abilities...then APPLY!

Scouts Canada Scholarship:

www.scouts.ca

Madd Canada Bursary Fund:

www.madd.ca

Chrysler Canada Inc. Scholarship Program:

www.cdnawards.com

Royal Bank Native Students Awards:

www.rbc.com

Ruth Hancock Memorial Scholarship:

www.cab-acr.ca

Terry Fox Humanitarian Award:

www.terryfox.org

Women's Opportunity Awards:

www.soroptimist.org

Award of Excellence Asthma Scholarships:

www.aaaai.org

Gloria Barron Prize for Young Heroes:

www.barronprize.org

John Gyles Education Awards:

www.johngyleseducationcenter.com

Canadian Nurses Foundation Scholarships:

www.cnf-fiic.ca

Wal-Mart Canada Scholarships:

www.walmart.ca

Learning Matters:

www.cst.org

Dropping Knowledge On Ya!

Translation: Sharing Some Interesting Facts About Canada

→ The Government of Canada offers a free guide outlining the services available for Seniors at:

www.servicecanada.gc.ca

→ Tired of working for people? Want to start your own business? Don't know how to get started? Canada Business is a government service that will assist entrepreneurs like you! Call 1-888-576-4444 or visit:

www.canadabusiness.ca

Education

I never thought there would be a day when I was celebrating school and education. When I found these amazing freebies, especially the HP freebie, it was very exciting because I know many people who pay a lot of money to get training on things like Microsoft Office and Web Design.

These courses won't make you an expert but you will walk away from each program way more informed and hopefully interested in continuing your learning through other channels.

OMG, I'm beginning to sound like a teacher — class dismissed!

→ HP Learning Centre

HP provides free online classes that are available 24 hours a day. This site is unbelievable; you can enroll in courses like Microsoft Office (Excel, PowerPoint, Word and Project), Adobe Photoshop, Web Design and Computer Security. They also include business skills courses related to marketing, organizing and managing your email inbox more effectively.

Consider this one a big gift, visit:

www.hp.com/go/learningcenter

to get da ultimate hookup.

→ Academic Earth

Did you go to an Ivy League School? Are you asking yourself, what is an Ivy League School?

I feel your pain. I think the majority of us are just trying to get through the day and don't have time to think about fancy schools that charge $100,000 per degree.

I worked with a guy that always said "you don't know, what you don't know." Every time I learn something new, I think about that guy. I'm not ashamed to say I think of that guy very often because I am literally always learning.

Academic Earth is an organization committed to providing everyone with access to a world-class education. They want regular people like you and me to be "in the know."

If you are interested in getting into the minds of the world's top scholars, this is a freebie you will love.

To view video lectures from universities like Harvard, Yale and Stanford, visit:

www.academicearth.org

→ Free University Education

A free university education from the Massachusetts Institute of Technology (MIT) sounds great. So what's the catch? No degree!

MIT launched their OpenCourseWare program in 2002 with 50 free courses and they now offer over 1800 free courses in a variety of languages. The program reports they are receiving over 2 million visits each month and content is also being added on YouTube and iTunes U.

This program does not require registration and you will gain access to lecture notes, exams and videos.

Check it out at:

http://ocw.mit.edu

@ Play

Entertainment

→ Video Games

Whether or not you are a true gamer, you have to pay tribute to one of the first gaming systems — Atari.

When you visit:

www.atari.com

you will gain access to games like Asteroids, Centipede, Scrabble, Monopoly, Gravitar and Missile Command.

If you've never heard of some of these games, be sure to have a look at how it all started. It's like going to the museum.

→ Museums

Speaking of museums, a great way to educate and entertain oneself is to spend some time at a local museum. Many museums offer free public access at certain times or on special days of the week. In some cases, free tickets are given to individuals or groups of very limited means.

For instance, the Royal Ontario Museum provides free admission every Wednesday from 4:30pm to 5:30pm. To find out what museums are in your area, check out the Canadian Museums Association's Directory of Museums at:

www.museums.ca/en/info_resources/canadas_museums

→ Music

If you love music then you need to know about LastFM. LastFM is a music service that offers tons of downloads every week for free! This service also tracks your listening habits, prepares your profile and can connect you with other listeners who share your musical tastes. Visit:

www.lastfm.com

itunes:

www.iTunes.com

is another great place to get free entertaining video and audio programs (podcasts).

TV SHOWS

(Warning...this section has major US Content!)

→ Canadian Shows

I've never felt a strong desire to sit in a studio audience and watch the live taping of a television show until I found out the tickets were free and the shows will often give you a parting gift. To get the 411 on your favourite show, contact the television station online or by calling.

Here are a few shows that are sure to educate and entertain:

The Hour hosted by George Stroumboulopoulos. This Canadian late night talk show is first-rate. 'Stroumbo' gets the best guests from around the world and they discuss issues and events that matter to Canadians. The Hour is filmed in downtown Toronto every Monday to Thursday from 4:30pm – 5:30pm. To get free tickets, visit:

www.cbc.ca/thehour/content/tickets.html

This Hour Has 22 Minutes offers Canadian comedy at its finest — every episode will leave you in stitches. They tape live on Monday evenings in Halifax. To get tickets, call 902-420-4765 or visit:

www.cbc.ca/22minutes

CityLine is a show that appeals to people interested in home decorating, fashion, cooking and gardening (to name a few). They tape all week at 299 Queen Street West in Toronto, Ontario and visitors can only attend one taping each year. To check them out, visit:

www.cityline.ca

→ US Shows

If you have a vacation planned for Los Angeles, New York or Chicago, you may want to visit your favourite TV show. Most people don't know that these tickets are free — if you ask.

The top two companies that distribute tickets are Audiences Unlimited and Audience Associates.

Audiences Unlimited can be reached online at:

www.tvtickets.com

or 1-818-260-0041. They offer tickets to shows like Dr. Phil, The Doctors and The Price is Right.

Find Audience Associates online at:

www.tvtix.com

or by phone at 1-818-985-8811. They offer tickets to shows like Live with Regis and Kelly, Saturday Night Live and Jeopardy.

The great thing about many of the shows is not only are the tickets free but shows like Ellen and Oprah often give the audience free gifts for attending.

To get tickets to sit in the studio audience for the Oprah Show, call the Seat Reservation Line at 312-591-9222, Monday through Friday, between 9am and 5pm CST.

To get tickets for the Ellen Show, visit:

www.ellen.warnerbros.com/tickets

This will bring you to their online calendar and you can select the day you wish to attend and check for availability.

→ Disney

Can you believe this!

Disney is offering free admission on your birthday! Who could ask for a better gift? This offer applies to the Theme Parks of Walt Disney World or Disneyland Resort. Register your birthday with Disney online at:

http://disneyparks.disney.go.com

If you're not sure what Disney has to offer, order a free copy of the Disney Vacation Planning Kit by calling 407-934-7639.

Dropping Knowledge On Ya!

Translation: Sharing Some Interesting Facts About Canada

→ Our current Maple Leaf Canadian Flag was inaugurated February 15th, 1965.

Sports

Sports are such an important part of Canadian living. We certainly love our hockey, and basketball continues to grow in popularity. Sports like baseball, football and soccer also have a special place within our hearts.

Many of our favorite teams offer Fan Packs to recognize the ongoing commitment and support they receive from the fans. A Fan Pack typically includes a mixture of items like athlete pictures, stickers, magazines, game programs, writing tools (pen/pencil), magnets, key chains, team photos, mini-flags and the list goes on and on.

In my three years of researching, I learned that these programs are not always continuous and the types of gift items change with regular frequency. The way to get a Fan Pack delivered to your front door is very simple; just ask nicely via email, posted letter or phone.

Keep in mind, the answer could be "no, not at this time" and usually you'll be advised when to expect the Fan Packs to be available again.

There are several leagues and hundreds of teams. The best way to get information about your favourite team is to visit the league website and select the team link. Once on your preferred team's site, you can send a polite request for a Fan Pack to the e-mail address usually found on the contact page.

Hockey - Visit:

www.nhl.com

and select Teams Menu

Basketball - Visit:

www.nba.com

and select Teams Menu

Baseball - Visit:

www.mlb.com

and select Team Sites

Football - Visit:

www.nfl.com

and select Teams

Soccer - Visit:

www.mlsnet.com

and select graphic of your preferred team's crest

Lacrosse - Visit:

www.nll.com

and select Teams

For those without Internet access, here are the mailing addresses for several Canadian teams. Feel free to send a letter requesting a complimentary Fan Pack.

→ NHL

Calgary Flames
P.O. Box 1540 Stn. M.
Calgary, Alberta
T2P 3B9
Tel: 403-777-4646

Edmonton Oilers Hockey Club
11230 - 110 Street
Edmonton, Alberta
T5G 3H7
Tel: 780-414-4000

Montreal Canadiens
1275 St. Antoine Street West
Montreal, Quebec
H3C 5L2

The Montreal Canadiens' website emphasizes the importance of providing your complete mailing address when requesting a Fan Pack.

For online ordering, the link is:

canadiens.nhl.com/fr/index.html

click Contact Us at the bottom of the page and complete the form online.

Ottawa Senators Hockey Club / Scotiabank Place
1000 Palladium Drive
Ottawa, Ontario
K2V 1A5
Tel: 613-599-0250

Vancouver Canucks
800 Griffiths Way
Vancouver, British Columbia
V6B 6G1
Tel: 604-899-7400

Toronto Maple Leafs
c/o Maple Leaf Sports and Entertainment Ltd.
40 Bay Street
Suite 400
Toronto, Ontario
M5J 2X2

→ NBA

Toronto Raptors
Air Canada Centre
40 Bay Street
Toronto, Ontario
M5J 2X2

→ MLB

Toronto Blue Jays
1 Blue Jay Way, Ste 3200
Toronto, Ontario
M5N 1J1

Dropping Knowledge On Ya!

Translation: Sharing Some Interesting Facts About Canada

→ Canadian homeowners can receive grants of up to $5000 per unit by making energy efficient retrofits through the ecoENERGY program. Visit:

www.nrcan.gc.ca

- For general inquiries:
  1 800 O-Canada (1 800 622-6232)

  To order publications:
  1-800-387-2000

Travel

Canadians enjoy vacations. We regularly use our vacation time to visit the United States, hot spots in the Caribbean and romantic European destinations like Italy and France.

There is one amazing country that all Canadians should immediately place on their must-see list. This country offers an eclectic mix of things to enjoy such as hot spring pools, river rafting, jazz festivals, casinos, museums, sport fishing, kayaking, hiking trails, parks, cathedrals, breweries, wine tours, skiing and world-class golfing.

This place we all need to see from coast-to-coast is Canada.

Canada is made up of 13 distinct provinces and territories — if you haven't seen them all, you should make it a priority.

Why not make your next vacation a Canadian holiday? Get together with family and friends to coordinate a trip to a different province.

Each Canadian province/territory offers a free travel guide to potential visitors. My research uncovered that all provinces will mail you a travel guide or you can easily download these guides to your computer.

To get hooked up on a free travel guide check out the following contact info:

→ British Columbia

British Columbia is located in Western Canada and this province is known for its delightful scenery, active living and pleasurable resorts. Key hot spots include the Vancouver Art Gallery, Stanley Park, river rafting in the Kootenay Rockies and shopping on Robson Street.

To order your free travel guide call 1-800-HelloBC (1-800-435-5622) or order online at:

www.hellobc.com

→ Alberta

Alberta is the fourth largest province that boasts the largest shopping mall in North America. Alberta is known for its gorgeous national parks in Banff and Jasper. When you are planning a visit, you may want to visit during Calgary Stampede.

Get your free vacation guide by calling 1-800-ALBERTA (1-800-252-3782) or sign up online at:

www.travelalberta.com

→ Saskatchewan

Saskatchewan is a culturally diverse province that is home to over one million Canadians. Saskatchewan offers outdoor adventures, casinos, spas and key places to visit include the RCMP Heritage Centre, Regina Plains Museum and Globe Theatre, Saskatchewan's first professional theatre company.

To order your free Saskatchewan Travel Guide, call 1-877-2ESCAPE (1-877-237-2273) or get it online at:

www.sasktourism.com

→ Manitoba

When you visit:

www.travelmanitoba.com

you are greeted with the phrase, "Welcome to the unforgettable Manitoba." With over 120 public and private golf courses, soft sand beaches, fishing, campgrounds and the chance to see Polar Bears in action, Manitoba is happening. Order your free Manitoba Information Kit and Maps online at:

www.travelmanitoba.com

When you visit, be sure to go to The Forks, Riel House and the Royal Winnipeg Ballet.

→ Ontario

Ontario is the second largest province and home to over 12,000,000 Canadians. This culturally diverse province has a wide variety of major attractions. You won't want to miss the CN Tower, Aboriginal Experiences and the beloved Stratford Festival. To order your free Ontario Travel Guide, visit:

www.ontariotravel.net

→ Quebec

Quebec is huge! Did you know that it measures three times the size of France? While there are many unique qualities about Quebec, a most distinctive quality is that the majority of its people speak French or they are bilingual (French/English). This province has so much to offer whether it is skiing at Mont- Tremblant, visiting historic sites like Place Royale or attending the internationally acclaimed Montreal Jazz Festival — the experience will amaze you. To order your free travel kit, go to:

www.bonjourquebec.com

→ New Brunswick

The seaside province of New Brunswick has a population of over 700,000 people. This province offers an assortment of everything that is right with the world; beauty, variety, nature, and entertainment to name a few! Places to see include Hopewell Rocks, Kingsbrae Garden, Saint John City Market and the Fundy Trail Parkway. Order your free visitor guide at:

www.tourismnewbrunswick.ca

→ Nova Scotia

Nova Scotia is the south-eastern province known for high-tides, extraordinary cuisine and Celtic music. This scenic province is surrounded by water and like the other provinces and territories, they welcome visitors with open arms. The attractions include Peggy's Cove, Alexander Keith's Brewery, Pier 21 National Historic Site and Tidal Bore Rafting. Check out:

www.novascotia.com

to order your free travel guide.

→ Prince Edward Island

Located in the Gulf of St. Lawrence, Prince Edward Island is a beautiful province that offers salt-water beaches, spectacular golfing, and true relaxation. As our smallest and most-green province, PEI has several spots you won't want to miss. The Green Gables Heritage Place, Confederation Centre of the Arts, Charlottetown Waterfront and Acadian Museum are well worth the visit. To get a free copy of their latest island guide, go to:

www.gentleisland.com

→ Newfoundland And Labrador

Newfoundland and Labrador is the most eastern Canadian province and it has a lot to offer prospective vacationers. From historic lighthouses to exciting outdoor adventures like kayaking, trails and snowmobiling, there is no shortage of fun in this province. The Viking Trail and East Coast Trail will not disappoint; get your free traveller's guide by calling 1-800-563-6353 or visiting online at:

www.newfoundlandlabrador.com

→ Yukon

According to Travel Yukon, if you visit Yukon and stay awhile, you won't want to leave. Yukon offers wilderness parks, natural wonders and rich traditions of the First Nations people who make up almost one quarter of the Yukon population.

If you are a nature lover or sports enthusiast, get your free vacation planner by calling 1-800-661-0494 or order it online at:

www.travelyukon.com

With spots like Tombstone Park, Yukon Wildlife Preserve and Takhini Hot Springs, this may be the setting for your next holiday adventure.

→ Northwest Territories

The Northwest Territories has over 40,000 residents and half of the population is of Aboriginal descent. The main industries are mining, government and tourism.

Fun things to add to your list when in the Northwest Territories include visiting the Prince of Wales Northern Heritage Centre, Arctic Cruise, Aurora by Dogsled Tour and Thelon Wildlife Sanctuary. Order your free vacation guide online at:

www.spectacularnwt.com

→ Nunavut

Nunavut is Canada's untamed, unspoiled and newest territory. While large in size, this arctic territory has the smallest population of all the provinces and territories in Canada.

The majority of Nunavut's people are Inuit and the official languages include Inuktitut, English and French. When in Nunavut, you'll want to venture into the historic parks and trails. You won't want to miss the Arctic Watch Lodge where you can view whales, foxes, arctic birds and polar bears.

If you are looking for a unique and authentic vacation experience, Nunavut will certainly deliver the goods. Visit:

www.nunavuttourism.com

to order your free travel guide.

Gifts From Our Prime Minister & Governor General

The Prime Minister of Canada will give you a shout out when you reach a certain age or achieve a significant marital milestone. This freebie comes in the form of a congratulatory letter or a certificate — and it really means a lot to old people.

A congratulatory letter is sent on wedding anniversaries for people celebrating their 25th, 30th, 35th, 40th and 45th anniversary. A letter is also sent for significant birthdays such as your 65th and 70th birthday.

The PM will go beyond letters and break out the certificates for your 50th wedding anniversary (and up) and for your 75th birthday (and up).

This is a really great gift to get for loved ones who achieve these milestones. The government makes it very easy to receive a greeting by providing an offline and online method to make your request. It is in your best interest to make the request at least three weeks before the milestone date to ensure you receive your congratulatory letter or certificate on time.

→ Online

The Prime Minister has a dedicated website and the form to request a special greeting is found on this site. The website is:

www.pm.gc.ca

and the specific page for the greeting is:

www.pm.gc.ca/eng/pmgreetings.asp

→ Postal Services

The Prime Minister has a great team of professionals to support the PM office. There is a Coordinator in place to assist with these types of requests. Please send the Coordinator your request in writing if you do not have access to the Internet.

Coordinator
Congratulatory Message
Room 105 - Langevin Block
Ottawa, Ontario, K1A 0A2

→ Gifts From The Governor General

The Governor General will hook you up with a nice written message for Wedding anniversaries of 50 years or higher, and birthdays of 90 years or higher and special events.

Special events include things like your retirement after 40 years of service with your employer, volunteering for over 25 years and major family reunions.

To complete a request for a message from the Governor General, please visit the website:

www.gg.ca

The specific webpage for the request form can be found at:

www.gg.ca/forms/specmsg_e.html

Please note the Governor General's office requires a minimum of six weeks to prepare these types of messages.

Services

A service is something that is designed to help; it is a set of tasks performed to aid an individual, groups, countries etc.

In the purest form, a service assists us and in the long run, we benefit in some way, shape or form.

Unlike products, we are not dealing with physical goods and the best services I can think of relate to experiences. Going to the spa for a special treatment, getting a haircut, taking a training course or being counseled are all examples of services we regularly enjoy.

Here are my top 10 service freebies that will benefit all Canadians:

→ Life Coaching

There has been a lot of fanfare about life coaching in the media. Life Coaching is sometimes confused with therapy or counseling, so let's clear this up right away. Life Coaching is about working with a trained professional and regularly engaging in meaningful conversations. Working collaboratively, you will develop a plan and successfully achieve your goals.

All Life Coaches are not created equal. If you are considering working with a coaching professional, ensure they are accredited and affiliated with a governing organization like the International Coach Federation.

Most coaches offer a no-obligation introductory free session. To find a coach in your hometown, visit:

www.coachfederation.org

and use the Find a Coach tool on their main page.

In addition to face-to-face coaching, telephone coaching has also been rising in popularity. If you are interested in working with a coach from the comfort of your home or office, e-mail Excelovate at:

info@excelovate.com

→ Credit Report

Your credit report provides a history of how you manage your financial responsibilities. It is used by lenders to determine whether or not to approve your request for financing.

It is absolutely critical that you know what is on your credit report at all times. By reviewing this report on a regular basis you will be able to ensure the information is accurate and confirm that only authorized parties are gaining access to your private information.

The two leading credit reporting agencies in Canada are Equifax and TransUnion.

If you need your credit report immediately, Equifax and TransUnion both offer a paid service on their websites.

Alternatively, you have the right to get a free copy of your report. This is referred to as a consumer disclosure. To obtain your free report, you can call, write or visit their agencies in person.

Equifax allows you to download the form online at:

www.equifax.ca

– see the Contact Us page or call 1-800-465-7166

Equifax Canada Inc.
Box 190 Jean Talon Station
Montreal, Quebec
H1S 2Z2

Tel: 1-800-465-7166
www.equifax.ca

TransUnion provides the Consumer Disclosure form online at:

www.transunion.ca

They also provide an in-person service where you can visit their offices in Newfoundland, Nova Scotia, Ontario, Prince Edward Island and Quebec.

Newfoundland	709-754-3992
Nova Scotia	902-429-1936
Ontario	800-663-9980
Prince Edward Island	902-368-1299
Quebec	877-713-3393

With identity thefts on the rise, we all need to take an active role in managing our personal information more effectively.

→ Dating

There are many online dating services but there is one that is worthy of mentioning. It was developed by a Canadian and is used by millions of people worldwide.

This online dating site was created by a gentleman named Markus and he created it because he saw the need to provide something that was 100% free and very people-focused. There are no charges whatsoever, not after 30 days, not after 60 days...it is absolutely free.

If you are looking for a way to meet people, check out Plenty of Fish online at:

www.plentyoffish.com

or

www.pof.com

→ Legal

Are you in the middle of a legal issue? Do you have a healthy curiosity and want to gain a better understanding of a legal matter? Look no further, Legal Line is a Canadian not-for-profit organization providing free legal information to Canadians by phone, fax and online at:

www.legalline.ca

It is important to note that Legal Line provides information — not advice.

With over 1000 topics in their database, this is a company that provides a service that all Canadians will need at some point in their lives.

Legal Line can be reached by telephone at 416-929-8400 and they also offer free guides to individuals and organizations.

Another great legal service in Canada is CanLaw. CanLaw is a free lawyer referral service for all Canadians. With over 65,000 lawyers in their database, this great service will put you in touch with an expert that is ready, willing and able to help. In most cases, these lawyers will provide a free half-hour consultation. When searching for a lawyer, visit:

www.canlaw.com

→ Recycling

Everyone has heard of recycling but have you heard of Freecycling? The Freecycle Network is a non-profit movement focused on keeping usable items out of our landfills.

Instead of throwing things away, millions of people are giving items like musical instruments, appliances and bicycles for free to people within their communities. Visit:

www.freecycle.org

to search for free items available in your area. This is a great site because it allows you to list items you need.

With over six million people already participating in the freecycle movement, it reminds me that there are a lot of great people in this world.

The next time you think of throwing something out, remember that it would feel a lot better to freecycle it.

→ Taxes

Don't pay to get your taxes done! QuickTax offers a free online tax preparation service for people who are comfortable with preparing their own taxes.

If you have a basic tax return — for instance, only T4 slips and no RRSPs, donations, investment income or medical expenses — this might be a great solution for you. This free tool is also available for students and people earning less than $20,000 per year. Check it out at:

www.quicktax.intuit.ca

→ Debt Management

Credit counseling is available for Canadians who need help managing their debts.

Many organizations will provide free credit counseling to struggling individuals and families. This counseling will help Canadians get their finances under control, develop a long-term debt-management plan and in some cases, the counselors will negotiate with creditors on your behalf.

For more details, visit:

www.moneyproblems.ca

or call 1-866-816-6547.

→ Social Networking

I think it is impossible to feel lonely in this day and age.

If you have a computer and never leave your bedroom, you can still be quite popular in certain social circles.

I am referring to the online communities that continue to grow exponentially. There is something for everyone in the world of social networking.

If you are looking for a free and fun way to socialize, check out my list of top 10 social networking sites:

WEBSITE	URL	DETAILS
MySpace	www.mySpace.com	Open – 14+
Facebook	www.facebook.com	Open – 13+
Black Planet	www.blackplanet.com	Open
Linkedin	www.linkedin.com	Open – 18+
Reunion	www.reunion.com	Open
Friendster	www.friendster.com	Open – 16+
Windows Live Spaces	www.spaces.live.com	Open to Everyone
Nexopia	www.nexopia.com	Canadian Youth
Habbo	www.habbo.com	Teens
Meetup	www.meetup.com	Open – 18+

→ Parental Training

The Nobody's Perfect program assists new parents with children five years old and under. By providing education and support, this program offered by the Public Health Agency of Canada will benefit low-income families with limited access to community resources.

For more details, call 1-613-952-1220
or email:

DCA_public_inquiries@phac-aspc.gc.ca

→ Language Training

The Language Instruction for Newcomers to Canada (LINC) program is geared to adults who are permanent residents. This program offers free language courses in English and French. For more information, call 1-888-242-2100.

Dropping Knowledge On Ya!

Translation: Sharing Some Interesting Facts About Canada

→ Are you planning any renovations like remodelling a kitchen/bathroom, installing new flooring, painting your home or laying down new sod? If so, you are probably eligible for a Home Renovation Tax Credit. The maximum credit is $1350 for more details call 613-995-2855 or visit:

www.cra-arc.gc.ca

Products

Believe it or not, many companies will give you their products for free. If you know anything about business, then you know that business people are out to make a profit. It is in their best interest to offer free gifts, samples or trials because if you like it, you will buy it and become a paying customer.

There was a time when you would have to write a sappy letter almost begging for a free sample. These days, a company will send you something based on your courteous request by phone or email. Amazingly, a lot of companies have online forms that make the process even easier!

Some people spend a lot of their time requesting anything and everything from companies and they end up with a house full of junk they'll never use. I've compiled a list of my top eight free product offers that are worth your time and energy.

Another thing to keep in mind is that many companies offer their free products for a limited time. If your request is declined don't let that deter you as there is usually another offer just around the corner. You can be assured that companies are always looking at new and innovative products to roll out to regular folks like you and me.

→ Mia Bella Scented Candles

All candles are not created equal. Do you know if the candles in your home are made with metal cores like lead and zinc? If so, you may be impacting your health and not even know it. The Mia Bella Scented Candle is a cleaner-burning option that is 90% soot free and the wax is made of all natural renewable materials.

Otanner Candles is a Canadian Distributor for Scent-Sations Inc., the makers of Mia Bella Candles. Otanner Candles will send you free samples to experience what they call "the best cleaner-burning scented candle in the world."

To receive a free sample delivered to your home, send an e-mail with your contact details to:

info@otanner.com

and they will provide you with a catalogue, a candle sample and information related to their Candle Of The Month Club.

Check out their website at:

www.otanner.com

→ Craigslist

Craigslist is a free online classified website that is community moderated. What does that mean? It's like everyone on your block putting a table in front of their home and selling or giving stuff away. You will need to specify your community and remember that the free stuff link can be found in the "For Sale" section — ironic, don't you think?

In addition to products, they also provide link-ups relating to jobs, romance, housing and local community events.

Craigslist can be found online at:

www.craigslist.com

I checked out Craigslist today and here are the types of things that I found listed on the free page:

- Computer Monitor
- Washer & Dryer
- Freezer
- Glass Table
- Black Desk
- 2 Lamps
- Dishwasher
- Microwave Oven
- Toaster
- 32" Television
- King Size Mattress
- Books
- Sofa Bed
- Baby Clothes
- Guitar

Craigslist is wicked! Craigslist is insane! I mean this all in the positive sense. If you love a hookup, you need to be down with Craigslist.

→ Proctor & Gamble (P&G)

According to their website, P&G products touch the lives of individuals three billion times a day. To give you an idea of who they are, here are some of their brands; Downy, Pantene, Cover Girl, Crest, Always, Duracell, Tide, Olay and Cascade.

P&G provide solutions for everyday living and as the leader in their industry; they frequently offer free products and samples.

Canadian residents can visit their website at:

www.pg.ca

to sign up for the mailing lists. They occasionally have special programs for free samples or discount coupons. Visit:

www.brandsampler.ca

or

www.brandsaver.ca

to sign up.

At the time of printing, both programs were suspended due to overwhelming demand. This is a good example of a company you need to be checking many times throughout the year so you don't miss out on these great opportunities.

→ The Holy Bible

Many people have heard of The Holy Bible but can you define it? Why is The Holy Bible so important to so many people and does it have a role in your life? This collection of sacred writings and scriptures are treasured by countless people around the globe. Many use The Holy Bible for guidance, support and to learn about God and his teachings.

I asked a dear friend who is very spiritual why she uses the bible and she said "The Bible is God's word and its guides me, instructs me, and inspires me in every aspect of my life."

Sign up for your free copy of the Holy Bible — King James Version. Visit online at:

www.freebiblesociety.org

or send a simple email request to:

freebiblesociety@gmail.com

It is important to note that the Bible Society will send you a free Bible and they will not visit you or follow up in any way.

→ Free Books, CDs, DVDs and Internet Access!!!!

There is a place in almost every Canadian community where you can go and get free books, CDs, and DVDs. As an added bonus, where available, you can also surf the Internet for free. Can you guess where this is?

That's right, the local library!

If you are serious about looking for free things and want to save your money, the library has all you need when it comes to products that will truly entertain you and your family at an affordable price.

If you found my book in the library, I think that is excellent! According to the Canadian Library Association, approximately two-thirds of Canadians already have a library card. That means 21 million of us are ready, willing and able to benefit right away!

C'mon Canadians, let's use the many great services Canada has to offer. As our money gets tighter, we have to be a little more creative in finding solutions.

When you visit your local library, remember to treat the library professionals with respect and take extra care with the materials you borrow — we are all in this together.

→ Contact Lenses

Johnson & Johnson Vision Care Canada markets the Acuvue brand contact lenses. Acuvue is the top contact lens brand worldwide and you can get a free trial pair of contact lenses. Visit:

www.acuvue.ca

to sign-up or go see your eye care professional for assistance. This offer applies to prescription lenses only.

→ Cell Phones

No one should pay for a cell phone.

Why would you pay for something that you could get for free?

I recently got the latest i-Phone and I didn't pay a cent! All the major cell phone companies have free phone offers and it's not because you are the apple of their eye.

These companies don't want to date you — they are looking to marry you. They want a long-term relationship and they expect you to be faithful.

So, what's the catch? It's pretty simple. When you sign up for two to three years, the deal is sealed.

The likelihood of you not needing a phone in 2 to 3 years is unreal. As long as you are alive, you will be using your cell phone. So save your money, make sure you get a good contract and get yourself hooked-up on a free phone.

Check out the following sites to get the 411 on the latest offers:

Fido:

www.fido.ca

Telus:

www.telusmobility.com

Rogers:

www.shoprogers.com

Bell:

www.solomobile.ca

or

www.bellmobility.ca

→ Naturel Spa

Naturel is a Canadian-owned company that specializes in natural bath and body care products. Naturel will send a sample pack that may include items such as shea butter, cocoa butter, sea salts and body mist. Naturel uses organic raw materials to produce their exclusive line of beauty products.

To order your free sampler, send an email request to:

sales@naturelspa.ca

Technology

Technology is all about innovation and applying science to things like life, our environment and society on the whole.

Technology is at work when we use our minds and the natural resources around us to develop effective tools for everyone's benefit.

For example, the following technology freebies automate the way we write a letter, perform calculations and communicate with one another.

Not only are the best things in life free, in this case the best things in life are also much simpler.

→ Office Software

Do you need to prepare documents, spreadsheets and presentations? Perhaps you are looking for neat graphics or wish to track information in a database.

All these tools are available to you for free. OpenOffice offers open-source office software that can be downloaded free of charge at:

www.openoffice.org

It is reported that this software has been downloaded over 50 million times. Check out this new and economical alternative!

→ Anti-Virus Software

All computer owners must recognize the importance of protecting computer systems against security threats.

As the fourth largest vendor of anti-virus software, AVG has approximately 80 million active users worldwide and that number continues to grow.

To protect your system at an affordable price (free), visit:

www.free.avg.com

→ Skype

Skype is changing the way we communicate over distances near and far! Are you interested in making free long-distance phone and video calls over the Internet? Skype jumped onto the scene in 2003 and since then, their service is being used in almost every country you could imagine.

Encourage your family and friends to get on Skype and you will be able to make free Skype-to-Skype calls around the clock.

Visit:

www.skype.com

to download their free software and you can start using this free innovative service right away.

→ Computers

If you think it is impossible to get a free computer, you are wrong. As you've already read in this book,

www.craigslist.com

and

www.kijiji.com

are great places to start your search.

If you work with a charity, church, daycare or elderly facility, you may want to check out the Electronics Recycling Association at:

www.era.ca

Finally, there is a wonderful program that collects, refurbishes and distributes computers to young children with a demonstrated need.

The program currently operates in Toronto but has goals to expand throughout Canada.

For more information, visit:

www.littlegeeks.org

→ faxZero

My fax machine was acting up and I had to send an urgent fax out of province. I ran to my local copy shop and was able to send the fax for $5.00. They were really nice to me and I got the job done on time. A few days later, I found out about faxZero, the company that allows you to send faxes for free in Canada and the US.

What!?! I lost my time, my gas and my five bucks.

If you have a few pages that need to be sent and you don't need to fax more than two times per day, this service is sweet. Look into this by visiting:

www.faxzero.com

→ Free Website

Interested in starting your own business? Want to learn how to build your own website? Excellent! The folks at yola.com offer a free tool that is extremely easy and requires absolutely no experience — just common sense. The difference between Yola and other companies is that there are no hidden fees and your site won't have any unwanted advertisements. Get started at:

www.yola.com

→ Web Conferencing Service

Dimdim provides a free tool that lets you collaborate online with up to 20 people around the world.

This free web conferencing service will save you time and money while working from the comfort of your home or office. With features such as sharing your desktop, broadcasting via webcam and delivering presentations, this is a dream solution worth looking into. Visit:

www.dimdim.com

Dropping Knowledge On Ya!

Translation: Sharing Some
Interesting Facts About Canada

→ Is your family prepared for an
emergency? Get your Emergency
Preparedness Guide at:

**www.preparez-vous.ca/prod/
ord/ordpub-eng.aspx**

and visit:

www.getprepared.ca

→ The Government of Canada offers
a free Guide outlining the services
available for Veterans at:

www.servicecanada.gc.ca/

Business

SMALL BUSINESS HOOKUP

I love business — it's exciting, rewarding and so very challenging.

What makes a small business so special is something you don't tend to see in large corporations — passion.

Talk to a small business owner about their new idea or innovation and you will immediately see the glee in their eyes and purpose in their stride.

Small business owners want to connect with people, make a difference, and do things that seem absolutely impossible. The following four hookups are specifically meant to help the little guy, hopefully, in a big way.

→ Guru

Are you a business professional looking for affordable help? Guru.com is a free service that will connect you with experts in areas such as web design, marketing, finance, legal, graphic design, sales and administration.

Guru is a vast online marketplace for freelance talent and you will be introduced to professionals locally, nationally and internationally.

Guru will hook you up with great talent for free. It is a quick and easy service that allows you to post a project, set a budget and collect bids from freelancers around the globe.

Once you award your project, you will be comforted in knowing that payment takes place only when you are 100% satisfied with the results. Visit:

www.guru.com

to register for a free membership.

You'll be amazed by two things; how many Canadians are doing business on guru.com and how much money you will save by using this amazing free service.

→ TED

What is leadership? What is thought leadership?
What is TED.com?

All great questions, I will answer one.

TED.com is where you need to go to hear some of the greatest minds of our time spend 18 minutes giving the talk of their lives.

Whether you are an established leader or an up-and-comer, TED.com needs to be a staple in your daily knowledge diet.

Technology, Entertainment, Design (TED) launched their annual conference in 1984 with the mission of bringing people together. They generously share their best talks and performances with the public for free.

Visit:

www.TED.com

to get inspired, to motivate your workforce and most importantly, to keep informed about the things that matter.

→ TJ Solutions Business Consulting

TJ Solutions is a Canadian Business Consulting Firm committed to working with new and existing business leaders. With over 15 years of experience, TJ Solutions delivers world-class strategies for corporations, non-profits, youth entrepreneurs and independent artists.

This full-service firm offers a free one hour consultation to assist with launching, funding and growing your business operation.

To book your consultation, visit:

www.tjsolutions.net

or call 1-866-542-6024.

→ HP Business Kit Templates

If you are thinking of starting your own business or if you're currently a small business owner, chances are, you don't have a Marketing Department.

HP offers a wide array of free business templates that will help you convey a polished and professional image to your customers. This valuable tool will allow you to create business cards, letterhead, newsletters and brochures. Visit HP online at:

www.hp.com/sbso/productivity/office

to get your business off to a great start.

Hustling

According to the Urban Dictionary, hustling is about making money by any means necessary. If you are short on cash and looking for legal ways to make some money, this chapter is for you.

Shockingly, there are a lot of ways to make extra money with programs such as Cash for Gold:

www.gold4cash.ca

Ebay:

www.ebay.ca

and Craigslist:

www.craigslist.ca

If you have items to sell, these three companies may be the right choice for you.

If you don't have items to sell, here are five proven ways you can make some honest cash and have a little fun in the process.

→ Mystery Shopping

Mystery Shoppers visit stores and perform investigative duties such as evaluating service levels or asking questions in order to report if employees are responding appropriately to customer inquiries. In return for these activities, mystery shoppers are awarded cash, discounts and free products.

There are many organizations that operate in Canada and in many cases the assignments are few and far between. The following organizations are very reputable and always looking for new, reliable shoppers.

Beyond Hello:

www.beyondhello.com

Intellishop:

www.intelli-shop.com

Premier Service Inc.:

www.premierservice.ca

CRG Mystery Shopping:

www.crgms.com

Tell Us About Us, Inc.:

www.tellusaboutus.com

→ Online Surveys

There are many companies that will pay you to understand your preferences relating to various products and services. The information received is used to make products more effective and services more desirable. There are many agencies that say they offer survey opportunities and you will see many online ads requesting money to sign you up for surveys. DO NOT PAY ANYONE TO DO SURVEYS. Reputable firms will not charge you — they will pay you. The following six companies are my top picks for firms worth your time:

Mindfield Online:

www.mindfieldonline.com

Survey Lion:

www.surveylion.com

Global Test Market:

www.globaltestmarket.com

Opinion Outpost:

www.opinionoutpost.com

Web Perspectives:

www.webperspectives.ca

Your 2 Cents:

www.your2cents.com

Keep in mind that you won't get rich quick by doing these surveys but you will make a little extra money while getting the chance to provide input and feedback.

→ Market Research Focus Groups

In addition to online surveys, there are a lot of market research organizations that will invite you to a nearby office to participate in focus groups.

In my area, there are three that I find to be excellent; Metroline, Quality Response and The Research House.

If you are located in Toronto, you may want to sign up for:

Metroline:

www.metroline.ca

Quality Response:

www.qualityresponse.ca/recruiting.html

or Research House:

www.research-house.ca

To find an organization in your area, visit the website for the Market Research and Intelligence Association at:

www.mria-arim.com

to check their Corporate Membership Directory and search for a firm in your city and/or province.

→ Teach English

Become an Odyssey Language Assistant and earn $2000 per month. This government program offers the opportunity to travel as well as teach English in provinces like Quebec and New Brunswick.

If English is your first language, you are a Canadian citizen and you've completed at least one year of post-secondary studies, this may be right up your alley.

Visit:

www.monodyssee.ca

for more details or to complete your application.

→ Get a Job

When all is said and done, hustling may not be the only way you wish to earn money. Getting a job is a more traditional approach to making ends meet that shouldn't be ruled out.

Many will search their local or national newspapers for prospective jobs. There is a tool that every job seeker should be using in their search for the next big thing. The tool is Workopolis.

This career website was launched in 2000 and reportedly features more than 50,000 jobs per day.

As Canada's biggest job site, make it a priority to search:

www.workopolis.com

for employment opportunities.

@ Hookup

Da End

You've just been hooked up on over 150 high-quality freebies. Welcome to a new way of living! For all the latest hookups, make sure you visit us online at least once a week. Believe me when I say, "you don't want to miss out on these goodies."

You may have noticed that a lot of the best hookups are online. If you're one of those people who don't have access, there's still hope for you because we've got three ways to hook you up:

1. Friends and Family

You are bound to have relatives or friends with Internet access. Reach out to them by paying a social visit to their home or office and ask to use their computer system.

2. Library

I cannot emphasize the amazing and important role of our community libraries. The library used to be my favourite spot in the world until I discovered the shopping mall. The point is that libraries tend to have Internet connected computers available for free public use.

3. Da Ultimate Hookup:

If you're absolutely out of options and don't want to miss out on these amazing freebies, give us a call and we will set you up — it will be a low-cost hookup. Just dial 416-619-5309.

For all the latest in "free things," make sure you stay in touch by checking us out online, participating in the weekly Hundred Dollar Hookup and joining our mailing list at:

www.daultimatehookup.com

Consider yourself officially hooked-up!

Add your own

If you find your own hookups note them down here for future use!

INDEX